MznLnx

Missing Links Exam Preps

Exam Prep for

Capital Markets

McInish, 1st Edition

The MznLnx Exam Prep is your link from the texbook and lecture to your exams.
The MznLnx Exam Preps are unauthorized and comprehensive reviews of your textbooks.

All material provided by MznLnx and Rico Publications (c) 2010
Textbook publishers and textbook authors do not particpate in or contribute to these reviews.

MznLnx

Rico
Publications

Exam Prep for Capital Markets
1st Edition
McInish

Publisher: Raymond Houge
Assistant Editor: Michael Rouger
Text and Cover Designer: Lisa Buckner
Marketing Manager: Sara Swagger
Project Manager, Editorial Production: Jerry Emerson
Art Director: Vernon Lowerui

Product Manager: Dave Mason
Editorial Assitant: Rachel Guzmanji
Pedagogy: Debra Long
Cover Image: Jim Reed/Getty Images
Text and Cover Printer: City Printing, Inc.
Compositor: Media Mix, Inc.

(c) 2010 Rico Publications
ALL RIGHTS RESERVED. No part of this work
covered by the copyright may be reproduced or
used in any form or by an means--graphic, electronic,
or mechanical, including photocopying, recording,
taping, Web distribution, information storage, and
retrieval systems, or in any other manner--without the
written permission of the publisher.

Printed in the United States
ISBN:

For more information about our products, contact us at:
Dave.Mason@RicoPublications.com

For permission to use material from this text or
product, submit a request online to:
Dave.Mason@RicoPublications.com

Contents

CHAPTER 1
FINANCIAL MARKETS AND THEIR PRODUCTS — 1

CHAPTER 2
SECONDARY MARKETS — 6

CHAPTER 3
TRANSACTION COSTS — 10

CHAPTER 4
CLEARING AND SETTLEMENT — 12

CHAPTER 5
REGULATION — 14

CHAPTER 6
EQUITIES — 16

CHAPTER 7
DEBT SECURITIES — 20

CHAPTER 8
DEBT SECURITIES: THEORETICAL CONSIDERATIONS — 22

CHAPTER 9
INTERNATIONAL PARITY RELATIONSHIPS — 26

CHAPTER 10
FOREIGN EXCHANGE — 31

CHAPTER 11
MARKOWITZ AND THE CAPITAL ASSET PRICING MODEL — 34

CHAPTER 12
FUTURES — 38

CHAPTER 13
OPTIONS — 43

CHAPTER 14
SWAPS — 45

CHAPTER 15
HEDGING — 47

ANSWER KEY — 51

TO THE STUDENT

COMPREHENSIVE

The *MznLnx* Exam Prep series is designed to help you pass your exams. Editors at MznLnx review your textbooks and then prepare these practice exams to help you master the textbook material. Unlike study guides, workbooks, and practice tests provided by the texbook publisher and textbook authors, *MznLnx* gives you **all** of the material in each chapter in exam form, not just samples, so you can be sure to nail your exam.

MECHANICAL

The MznLnx Exam Prep series creates exams that will help you learn the subject matter as well as test you on your understanding. Each question is designed to help you master the concept. Just working through the exams, you gain an understanding of the subject--its a simple mechanical process that produces success.

INTEGRATED STUDY GUIDE AND REVIEW

MznLnx is not just a set of exams designed to test you, its also a comprehensive review of the subject content. Each exam question is also a review of the concept, making sure that you will get the answer correct without having to go to other sources of material. You learn as you go! Its the easiest way to pass an exam.

HUMOR

Studying can be tedious and dry. MznLnx's instructional design includes moderate humor within the exam questions on occassion, to break the tedium and revitalize the brain

Chapter 1. FINANCIAL MARKETS AND THEIR PRODUCTS

1. In economics, the _____ is the term economists use to describe the self-regulating nature of the marketplace. The _____ is a metaphor coined by the economist Adam Smith in The Wealth of Nations.

Adam Smith mentions the metaphor in Book IV of The Wealth of Nations, arguing that people in any society will certainly employ their capital in foreign trading only if the profits available by that method far exceed those available locally, and that in such a case it is better for society as a whole if they so did.

   a. ABN Amro
   b. Invisible hand
   c. AAB
   d. A Random Walk Down Wall Street

2. _____ most frequently refers to the standard deviation of the continuously compounded returns of a financial instrument with a specific time horizon. It is often used to quantify the risk of the instrument over that time period. _____ is typically expressed in annualized terms, and it may either be an absolute number ($5) or a fraction of the mean (5%).
   a. Seasoned equity offering
   b. Portfolio insurance
   c. Volatility
   d. Currency swap

3. _____ is typically a higher ranking stock than voting shares, and its terms are negotiated between the corporation and the investor.

_____ usually carry no voting rights, but may carry superior priority over common stock in the payment of dividends and upon liquidation. _____ may carry a dividend that is paid out prior to any dividends to common stock holders.

   a. Second lien loan
   b. Trade-off theory
   c. Follow-on offering
   d. Preferred stock

4. _____ refers to a system of banking or banking activity that is consistent with the principles of Islamic law (Sharia) and its practical application through the development of Islamic economics. Sharia prohibits the payment of fees for the renting of money (Riba, usury) for specific terms, as well as investing in businesses that provide goods or services considered contrary to its principles (Haraam, forbidden.) While these principles were used as the basis for a flourishing economy in earlier times, it is only in the late 20th century that a number of Islamic banks were formed to apply these principles to private or semi-private commercial institutions within the Muslim community.

Chapter 1. FINANCIAL MARKETS AND THEIR PRODUCTS

a. A Random Walk Down Wall Street
b. AAB
c. ABN Amro
d. Islamic banking

5. A _____ or market-based mechanism is any of a wide variety of ways to match up buyers and sellers.

An example of a _____ uses announced bid and ask prices. Generally speaking, when two parties wish to engage in a trade, the purchaser will announce a price he is willing to pay (the bid price) and seller will announce a price he is willing to accept (the ask price).

a. 4-4-5 Calendar
b. 529 plan
c. 7-Eleven
d. Price mechanism

6. The _____ for securities is the difference between the price quoted by a market maker for an immediate sale and an immediate purchase The size of the bid-offer spread in a given commodity is a measure of the liquidity of the market.

The trader initiating the transaction is said to demand liquidity, and the other party to the transaction supplies liquidity.

a. Trade-off
b. Defined contribution plan
c. Capital outflow
d. Bid/offer spread

7. In economics, business, and accounting, a _____ is the value of money that has been used up to produce something, and hence is not available for use anymore. In business, the _____ may be one of acquisition, in which case the amount of money expended to acquire it is counted as _____. In this case, money is the input that is gone in order to acquire the thing.
a. Sliding scale fees
b. Fixed costs
c. Marginal cost
d. Cost

8. A _____ is a financial contract whose value is derived from the value of something else (known as the underlying.) The underlying on which a _____ is based can be an asset, weather conditions bonds or other forms of credit.

a. 4-4-5 Calendar
b. 529 plan
c. 7-Eleven
d. Derivative

9. In economics and related disciplines, a _____ is a cost incurred in making an economic exchange. For example, most people, when buying or selling a stock, must pay a commission to their broker; that commission is a _____ of doing the stock deal. Or consider buying a banana from a store; to purchase the banana, your costs will be not only the price of the banana itself, but also the energy and effort it requires to find out which of the various banana products you prefer, where to get them and at what price, the cost of traveling from your house to the store and back, the time waiting in line, and the effort of the paying itself; the costs above and beyond the cost of the banana are the _____s.
   a. Variable costs
   b. Transaction cost
   c. Fixed costs
   d. Marginal cost

10. In finance, a _____ is a security that entitles the holder to buy stock of the company that issued it at a specified price, which is usually higher than the stock price at time of issue.

    _____s are frequently attached to bonds or preferred stock as a sweetener, allowing the issuer to pay lower interest rates or dividends. They can be used to enhance the yield of the bond, and make them more attractive to potential buyers.

    a. Clearing house
    b. Clearing
    c. Warrant
    d. Credit

11. The term _____ refers to three closely related concepts:

    - The _____ model is a mathematical model of the market for an equity, in which the equity's price is a stochastic process.
    - The _____ PDE is a partial differential equation which (in the model) must be satisfied by the price of a derivative on the equity.
    - The _____ formula is the result obtained by solving the _____ PDE for a European call option.

Fischer Black and Myron Scholes first articulated the _____ formula in their 1973 paper, 'The Pricing of Options and Corporate Liabilities.' The foundation for their research relied on work developed by scholars such as Jack L. Treynor, Paul Samuelson, A. James Boness, Sheen T. Kassouf, and Edward O. Thorp. The fundamental insight of _____ is that the option is implicitly priced if the stock is traded.

Robert C. Merton was the first to publish a paper expanding the mathematical understanding of the options pricing model and coined the term '_____' options pricing model.

a. Perpetuity
b. Stochastic volatility
c. Modified Internal Rate of Return
d. Black-Scholes

12. An _____ is a contract written by a seller that conveys to the buyer the right -- but not the obligation -- to buy (in the case of a call _____) or to sell (in the case of a put _____) a particular asset, such as a piece of property such as, among others, a futures contract. In return for granting the _____, the seller collects a payment (the premium) from the buyer.

For example, buying a call _____ provides the right to buy a specified quantity of a security at a set strike price at some time on or before expiration, while buying a put _____ provides the right to sell.

a. AT'T Mobility LLC
b. Option
c. Amortization
d. Annuity

13. _____ refers to any type of investment that yields a regular (or fixed) return.

For example, if you lend money to a borrower and the borrower has to pay interest once a month, you have been issued a fixed-income security. When a company does this, it is often called a bond or corporate bank debt (although preferred stock is also sometimes considered to be _____).

a. 529 plan
b. 4-4-5 Calendar
c. Bond market
d. Fixed income

14. _____, refers to consumption opportunity gained by an entity within a specified time frame, which is generally expressed in monetary terms. However, for households and individuals, '_____ is the sum of all the wages, salaries, profits, interests payments, rents and other forms of earnings received... in a given period of time.' For firms, _____ generally refers to net-profit: what remains of revenue after expenses have been subtracted.

a. Accrual
b. Annual report
c. Income
d. OIBDA

15. A _____ is a fungible, negotiable instrument representing financial value. They are broadly categorized into debt securities (such as banknotes, bonds and debentures), and equity securities; e.g., common stocks. The company or other entity issuing the _____ is called the issuer.
   a. Tracking stock
   b. Book entry
   c. Securities lending
   d. Security

16. _____, is when a company issues common stock or shares to the public for the first time. They are often issued by smaller, younger companies seeking capital to expand, but can also be done by large privately-owned companies looking to become publicly traded.

In an _____ the issuer may obtain the assistance of an underwriting firm, which helps it determine what type of security to issue (common or preferred), best offering price and time to bring it to market.

   a. Asian Financial Crisis
   b. Insolvency
   c. Initial public offering
   d. Interest

17. In finance, _____ or 'shorting' is the practice of selling a financial instrument that the seller does not own at the time of the sale. _____ is done with intent of later purchasing the financial instrument at a lower price. Short-sellers attempt to profit from an expected decline in the price of a financial instrument.
   a. 4-4-5 Calendar
   b. 529 plan
   c. Short ratio
   d. Short selling

Chapter 2. SECONDARY MARKETS

1. _____ is a measure of the ability of a debtor to pay their debts as and when they fall due. It is usually expressed as a ratio or a percentage of current liabilities.

For a corporation with a published balance sheet there are various ratios used to calculate a measure of liquidity.

   a. Operating profit margin
   b. Invested capital
   c. Operating leverage
   d. Accounting liquidity

2. A _____ or market-based mechanism is any of a wide variety of ways to match up buyers and sellers.

An example of a _____ uses announced bid and ask prices. Generally speaking, when two parties wish to engage in a trade, the purchaser will announce a price he is willing to pay (the bid price) and seller will announce a price he is willing to accept (the ask price).

   a. 529 plan
   b. 7-Eleven
   c. Price mechanism
   d. 4-4-5 Calendar

3. The _____ for securities is the difference between the price quoted by a market maker for an immediate sale and an immediate purchase The size of the bid-offer spread in a given commodity is a measure of the liquidity of the market.

The trader initiating the transaction is said to demand liquidity, and the other party to the transaction supplies liquidity.

   a. Bid/offer spread
   b. Trade-off
   c. Defined contribution plan
   d. Capital outflow

4. In economics, business, and accounting, a _____ is the value of money that has been used up to produce something, and hence is not available for use anymore. In business, the _____ may be one of acquisition, in which case the amount of money expended to acquire it is counted as _____. In this case, money is the input that is gone in order to acquire the thing.

Chapter 2. SECONDARY MARKETS

a. Fixed costs
b. Marginal cost
c. Sliding scale fees
d. Cost

5. The _____ process is the process of determining the price of an asset in the marketplace through the interactions of buyers and sellers .

_____ is different from valuation. _____ process involves buyers and sellers arriving at a transaction price for a specific item at a given time.

a. Seed round
b. Return on capital employed
c. Pecking order theory
d. Price discovery

6. In economics and related disciplines, a _____ is a cost incurred in making an economic exchange. For example, most people, when buying or selling a stock, must pay a commission to their broker; that commission is a _____ of doing the stock deal. Or consider buying a banana from a store; to purchase the banana, your costs will be not only the price of the banana itself, but also the energy and effort it requires to find out which of the various banana products you prefer, where to get them and at what price, the cost of traveling from your house to the store and back, the time waiting in line, and the effort of the paying itself; the costs above and beyond the cost of the banana are the _____s.
a. Fixed costs
b. Marginal cost
c. Transaction cost
d. Variable costs

7. The _____ is one of several stock market indices, created by nineteenth-century Wall Street Journal editor and Dow Jones ' Company co-founder Charles Dow. Dow compiled the index to gauge the performance of the industrial sector of the American stock market. It is the second-oldest U.S. market index, after the Dow Jones Transportation Average, which Dow also created.
a. 4-4-5 Calendar
b. 529 plan
c. 7-Eleven
d. Dow Jones Industrial Average

8. _____ is an American publishing and financial information firm.

Chapter 2. SECONDARY MARKETS

The company was founded in 1882 by three reporters: Charles Dow, Edward Jones, and Charles Bergstresser. Like The New York Times and the Washington Post, the company was in recent years publicly traded but privately controlled.

   a. Dow Jones ' Company
   b. The Dun ' Bradstreet Corporation
   c. Federal National Mortgage Association
   d. Holding company

9. _____ most frequently refers to the standard deviation of the continuously compounded returns of a financial instrument with a specific time horizon. It is often used to quantify the risk of the instrument over that time period. _____ is typically expressed in annualized terms, and it may either be an absolute number ($5) or a fraction of the mean (5%).
   a. Portfolio insurance
   b. Seasoned equity offering
   c. Currency swap
   d. Volatility

10. An _____ is the term used in financial circles for a type of computer system that facilitates trading of financial products outside of stock exchanges. The primary products that are traded on an _____ are stocks and currencies. They came into existence in 1998 when the SEC authorized their creation.
   a. Intellidex
   b. Open outcry
   c. Insider trading
   d. Electronic communication network

11. In financial markets, a _____ is the smallest increment in which prices for a futures contract can move.
   a. CFA Institute
   b. Tick size
   c. Credit card balance transfer
   d. Collateralized loan obligation

12. In finance, a _____ is a trade that is usually at least 10,000 shares of a stock or $200,000 of bonds. It can also refer specifically to large trades that occur between institutional parties at a fixed price. For instance, an insurance company may hold a large stake in a company that they would like to liquidate completely.

Chapter 2. SECONDARY MARKETS

a. 4-4-5 Calendar
b. 529 plan
c. Block trade
d. 7-Eleven

13. The _____ is the financial market where previously issued securities and financial instruments such as stock, bonds, options, and futures are bought and sold. The term '_____' is also used refer to the market for any used goods or assets, or an alternative use for an existing product or asset where the customer base is the second market

With primary issuances of securities or financial instruments, or the primary market, investors purchase these securities directly from issuers such as corporations issuing shares in an IPO or private placement, or directly from the federal government in the case of treasuries.

a. Performance attribution
b. Financial market
c. Delta neutral
d. Secondary market

Chapter 3. TRANSACTION COSTS

1. A _____ or market-based mechanism is any of a wide variety of ways to match up buyers and sellers.

An example of a _____ uses announced bid and ask prices. Generally speaking, when two parties wish to engage in a trade, the purchaser will announce a price he is willing to pay (the bid price) and seller will announce a price he is willing to accept (the ask price).

   a. 529 plan
   b. Price mechanism
   c. 4-4-5 Calendar
   d. 7-Eleven

2. The _____ for securities is the difference between the price quoted by a market maker for an immediate sale and an immediate purchase The size of the bid-offer spread in a given commodity is a measure of the liquidity of the market.

The trader initiating the transaction is said to demand liquidity, and the other party to the transaction supplies liquidity.

   a. Defined contribution plan
   b. Trade-off
   c. Capital outflow
   d. Bid/offer spread

3. In economics, business, and accounting, a _____ is the value of money that has been used up to produce something, and hence is not available for use anymore. In business, the _____ may be one of acquisition, in which case the amount of money expended to acquire it is counted as _____. In this case, money is the input that is gone in order to acquire the thing.
   a. Fixed costs
   b. Marginal cost
   c. Sliding scale fees
   d. Cost

4. In economics and related disciplines, a _____ is a cost incurred in making an economic exchange. For example, most people, when buying or selling a stock, must pay a commission to their broker; that commission is a _____ of doing the stock deal. Or consider buying a banana from a store; to purchase the banana, your costs will be not only the price of the banana itself, but also the energy and effort it requires to find out which of the various banana products you prefer, where to get them and at what price, the cost of traveling from your house to the store and back, the time waiting in line, and the effort of the paying itself; the costs above and beyond the cost of the banana are the _____s.

a. Variable costs
b. Fixed costs
c. Marginal cost
d. Transaction cost

5. _____ are expenses that change in proportion to the activity of a business. In other words, _____ are the sum of marginal costs. It can also be considered normal costs. Along with fixed costs, _____ make up the two components of total cost. Direct Costs, however, are costs that can be associated with a particular cost object.
    a. Variable costs
    b. Cost accounting
    c. Fixed costs
    d. Transaction cost

6. A '_____' is a 'Charge' that is paid to obtain the right to delay a payment. Essentially, the payer purchases the right to make a given payment in the future instead of in the Present. The '_____', or 'Charge' that must be paid to delay the payment, is simply the difference between what the payment amount would be if it were paid in the present and what the payment amount would be paid if it were paid in the future.
    a. Discount
    b. Risk modeling
    c. Risk aversion
    d. Value at risk

Chapter 4. CLEARING AND SETTLEMENT

1. _____ refers to a system of banking or banking activity that is consistent with the principles of Islamic law (Sharia) and its practical application through the development of Islamic economics. Sharia prohibits the payment of fees for the renting of money (Riba, usury) for specific terms, as well as investing in businesses that provide goods or services considered contrary to its principles (Haraam, forbidden.) While these principles were used as the basis for a flourishing economy in earlier times, it is only in the late 20th century that a number of Islamic banks were formed to apply these principles to private or semi-private commercial institutions within the Muslim community.
    a. ABN Amro
    b. AAB
    c. Islamic banking
    d. A Random Walk Down Wall Street

2. In general, _____ means to allow a positive value and a negative value to set-off and partially or entirely cancel each other out.

In the context of credit risk, there are at least three specific types of _____:

- Close-out _____

- _____ by novation

- Settlement or payment _____

_____ decreases credit exposure, increases business with existing counterparties, and reduces both operational and settlement risk and operational costs.

   a. Moneylender
   b. Reinvestment risk
   c. Forward price
   d. Netting

3. _____ most frequently refers to the standard deviation of the continuously compounded returns of a financial instrument with a specific time horizon. It is often used to quantify the risk of the instrument over that time period. _____ is typically expressed in annualized terms, and it may either be an absolute number ($5) or a fraction of the mean (5%).
    a. Volatility
    b. Seasoned equity offering
    c. Currency swap
    d. Portfolio insurance

Chapter 4. CLEARING AND SETTLEMENT

4. In finance, a _____ is collateral that the holder of a position in securities, options, or futures contracts has to deposit to cover the credit risk of his counterparty (most often his broker.) This risk can arise if the holder has done any of the following:

- borrowed cash from the counterparty to buy securities or options,
- sold securities or options short, or
- entered into a futures contract.

The collateral can be in the form of cash or securities, and it is deposited in a _____ account. On U.S. futures exchanges, '_____' was formally called performance bond.

_____ buying is buying securities with cash borrowed from a broker, using other securities as collateral.

a. Share
b. Procter ' Gamble
c. Credit
d. Margin

5. A _____ is a financial services company that provides clearing and settlement services for financial transactions, usually on a futures exchange, and often acts as central counterparty (the payor actually pays the _____, which then pays the payee). A _____ may also offer novation, the substitution of a new contract or debt for an old, or other credit enhancement services to its members.

The term is also used for banks like Suffolk Bank that acted as a restraint on the over-issuance of private bank notes.

a. Valuation
b. Bucket shop
c. Warrant
d. Clearing house

Chapter 5. REGULATION

1. _____ refers to a system of banking or banking activity that is consistent with the principles of Islamic law (Sharia) and its practical application through the development of Islamic economics. Sharia prohibits the payment of fees for the renting of money (Riba, usury) for specific terms, as well as investing in businesses that provide goods or services considered contrary to its principles (Haraam, forbidden.) While these principles were used as the basis for a flourishing economy in earlier times, it is only in the late 20th century that a number of Islamic banks were formed to apply these principles to private or semi-private commercial institutions within the Muslim community.
   a. AAB
   b. ABN Amro
   c. Islamic banking
   d. A Random Walk Down Wall Street

2. _____ is a legally declared inability or impairment of ability of an individual or organization to pay their creditors. Creditors may file a _____ petition against a debtor ('involuntary _____') in an effort to recoup a portion of what they are owed or initiate a restructuring. In the majority of cases, however, _____ is initiated by the debtor (a 'voluntary _____' that is filed by the bankrupt individual or organization.)
   a. Debt settlement
   b. Bankruptcy
   c. 4-4-5 Calendar
   d. 529 plan

3. A _____ is a fungible, negotiable instrument representing financial value. They are broadly categorized into debt securities (such as banknotes, bonds and debentures), and equity securities; e.g., common stocks. The company or other entity issuing the _____ is called the issuer.
   a. Tracking stock
   b. Securities lending
   c. Security
   d. Book entry

4. A _____ is a financial contract whose value is derived from the value of something else (known as the underlying.) The underlying on which a _____ is based can be an asset, weather conditions bonds or other forms of credit.
   a. 4-4-5 Calendar
   b. 529 plan
   c. 7-Eleven
   d. Derivative

5. The _____ are the financial markets for derivatives. The market can be divided into two, that for exchange traded derivatives and that for over-the-counter derivatives. The legal nature of these products is very different as well as the way they are traded, though many market participants are active in both.

a. Notional amount
b. Commodity tick
c. Real estate derivatives
d. Derivatives markets

Chapter 6. EQUITIES

1. _____ refers to a system of banking or banking activity that is consistent with the principles of Islamic law (Sharia) and its practical application through the development of Islamic economics. Sharia prohibits the payment of fees for the renting of money (Riba, usury) for specific terms, as well as investing in businesses that provide goods or services considered contrary to its principles (Haraam, forbidden.) While these principles were used as the basis for a flourishing economy in earlier times, it is only in the late 20th century that a number of Islamic banks were formed to apply these principles to private or semi-private commercial institutions within the Muslim community.

   a. A Random Walk Down Wall Street
   b. Islamic banking
   c. ABN Amro
   d. AAB

2. _____ is a form of corporation equity ownership represented in the securities. It is dangerous in comparison to preferred shares and some other investment options, in that in the event of bankruptcy, _____ investors receive their funds after preferred stockholders, bondholders, creditors, etc. On the other hand, common shares on average perform better than preferred shares or bonds over time.

   a. Stock split
   b. Stock market bubble
   c. Stop-limit order
   d. Common stock

3. _____ is typically a higher ranking stock than voting shares, and its terms are negotiated between the corporation and the investor.

   _____ usually carry no voting rights, but may carry superior priority over common stock in the payment of dividends and upon liquidation. _____ may carry a dividend that is paid out prior to any dividends to common stock holders.

   a. Trade-off theory
   b. Preferred stock
   c. Follow-on offering
   d. Second lien loan

4. A _____ or market-based mechanism is any of a wide variety of ways to match up buyers and sellers.

An example of a _____ uses announced bid and ask prices. Generally speaking, when two parties wish to engage in a trade, the purchaser will announce a price he is willing to pay (the bid price) and seller will announce a price he is willing to accept (the ask price).

Chapter 6. EQUITIES

a. 7-Eleven
b. 4-4-5 Calendar
c. 529 plan
d. Price mechanism

5. The _____ for securities is the difference between the price quoted by a market maker for an immediate sale and an immediate purchase The size of the bid-offer spread in a given commodity is a measure of the liquidity of the market.

The trader initiating the transaction is said to demand liquidity, and the other party to the transaction supplies liquidity.

a. Trade-off
b. Bid/offer spread
c. Defined contribution plan
d. Capital outflow

6. In economics, business, and accounting, a _____ is the value of money that has been used up to produce something, and hence is not available for use anymore. In business, the _____ may be one of acquisition, in which case the amount of money expended to acquire it is counted as _____. In this case, money is the input that is gone in order to acquire the thing.

a. Marginal cost
b. Sliding scale fees
c. Fixed costs
d. Cost

7. In economics and related disciplines, a _____ is a cost incurred in making an economic exchange. For example, most people, when buying or selling a stock, must pay a commission to their broker; that commission is a _____ of doing the stock deal. Or consider buying a banana from a store; to purchase the banana, your costs will be not only the price of the banana itself, but also the energy and effort it requires to find out which of the various banana products you prefer, where to get them and at what price, the cost of traveling from your house to the store and back, the time waiting in line, and the effort of the paying itself; the costs above and beyond the cost of the banana are the _____s.

a. Variable costs
b. Fixed costs
c. Transaction cost
d. Marginal cost

8. In finance, a _____ is a security that entitles the holder to buy stock of the company that issued it at a specified price, which is usually higher than the stock price at time of issue.

Chapter 6. EQUITIES

_____s are frequently attached to bonds or preferred stock as a sweetener, allowing the issuer to pay lower interest rates or dividends. They can be used to enhance the yield of the bond, and make them more attractive to potential buyers.

a. Clearing
b. Warrant
c. Credit
d. Clearing house

9. _____ is a stock market index for the Tokyo Stock Exchange (TSE.) It has been calculated daily by the Nihon Keizai Shimbun (Nikkei) newspaper since 1950. It is a price-weighted average (the unit is Yen), and the components are reviewed once a year.
a. Nikkei 225
b. 7-Eleven
c. 4-4-5 Calendar
d. 529 plan

10. An _____ or index tracker is a collective investment scheme (usually a mutual fund or exchange-traded fund) that aims to replicate the movements of an index of a specific financial market regardless of market conditions.

Tracking can be achieved by trying to hold all of the securities in the index, in the same proportions as the index. Other methods include statistically sampling the market and holding 'representative' securities.

a. AAB
b. A Random Walk Down Wall Street
c. Index fund
d. Investment company

11. In finance, a _____ is a position established in one market in an attempt to offset exposure to the price risk of an equal but opposite obligation or position in another market -- usually, but not always, in the context of one's commercial activity. Hedging is a strategy designed to minimize exposure to such business risks as a sharp contraction in demand for one's inventory, while still allowing the business to profit from producing and maintaining that inventory. A typical hedger might be a farmer with 2000 acres of unharvested wheat in the ground, who would rather tend his crop without the distraction of uncertain prices.

Chapter 6. EQUITIES

a. 529 plan
b. 7-Eleven
c. 4-4-5 Calendar
d. Hedge

12. A _____ is a private investment fund open to a limited range of investors that is permitted by regulators to undertake a wider range of activities than other investment funds and also pays a performance fee to its investment manager. Each fund will have its own strategy which determines the type of investments and the methods of investment it undertakes. _____s as a class invest in a broad range of investments extending over shares, debt, commodities and beyond.

a. 7-Eleven
b. 529 plan
c. 4-4-5 Calendar
d. Hedge fund

13. _____ refers to the likelihood that changes in the business environment adversely affect operating profits or the value of assets in a specific country. For example, financial factors such as currency controls, devaluation or regulatory changes, or stability factors such as mass riots, civil war and other potential events contribute to companies' operational risks. This term is also sometimes referred to as political risk, however _____ is a more general term, which generally only refers to risks affecting all companies operating within a particular country.

a. Capital asset
b. Solvency
c. Single-index model
d. Country risk

Chapter 7. DEBT SECURITIES

1. _____ refers to a system of banking or banking activity that is consistent with the principles of Islamic law (Sharia) and its practical application through the development of Islamic economics. Sharia prohibits the payment of fees for the renting of money (Riba, usury) for specific terms, as well as investing in businesses that provide goods or services considered contrary to its principles (Haraam, forbidden.) While these principles were used as the basis for a flourishing economy in earlier times, it is only in the late 20th century that a number of Islamic banks were formed to apply these principles to private or semi-private commercial institutions within the Muslim community.
   a. AAB
   b. A Random Walk Down Wall Street
   c. ABN Amro
   d. Islamic banking

2. The _____ is one of several stock market indices, created by nineteenth-century Wall Street Journal editor and Dow Jones ' Company co-founder Charles Dow. Dow compiled the index to gauge the performance of the industrial sector of the American stock market. It is the second-oldest U.S. market index, after the Dow Jones Transportation Average, which Dow also created.
   a. 529 plan
   b. 7-Eleven
   c. 4-4-5 Calendar
   d. Dow Jones Industrial Average

3. In finance, the _____ is the global financial market for short-term borrowing and lending. It provides short-term liquidity funding for the global financial system. The _____ is where short-term obligations such as Treasury bills, commercial paper and bankers' acceptances are bought and sold.
   a. Debt-for-equity swap
   b. Consumer debt
   c. Cramdown
   d. Money market

4. _____ most frequently refers to the standard deviation of the continuously compounded returns of a financial instrument with a specific time horizon. It is often used to quantify the risk of the instrument over that time period. _____ is typically expressed in annualized terms, and it may either be an absolute number ($5) or a fraction of the mean (5%).
   a. Seasoned equity offering
   b. Currency swap
   c. Portfolio insurance
   d. Volatility

Chapter 7. DEBT SECURITIES

5. The term _____ refers to three closely related concepts:

   - The _____ model is a mathematical model of the market for an equity, in which the equity's price is a stochastic process.
   - The _____ PDE is a partial differential equation which (in the model) must be satisfied by the price of a derivative on the equity.
   - The _____ formula is the result obtained by solving the _____ PDE for a European call option.

Fischer Black and Myron Scholes first articulated the _____ formula in their 1973 paper, 'The Pricing of Options and Corporate Liabilities.' The foundation for their research relied on work developed by scholars such as Jack L. Treynor, Paul Samuelson, A. James Boness, Sheen T. Kassouf, and Edward O. Thorp. The fundamental insight of _____ is that the option is implicitly priced if the stock is traded.

Robert C. Merton was the first to publish a paper expanding the mathematical understanding of the options pricing model and coined the term '_____' options pricing model.

   a. Stochastic volatility
   b. Perpetuity
   c. Modified Internal Rate of Return
   d. Black-Scholes

6. An _____ is a contract written by a seller that conveys to the buyer the right -- but not the obligation -- to buy (in the case of a call _____) or to sell (in the case of a put _____) a particular asset, such as a piece of property such as, among others, a futures contract. In return for granting the _____, the seller collects a payment (the premium) from the buyer.

For example, buying a call _____ provides the right to buy a specified quantity of a security at a set strike price at some time on or before expiration, while buying a put _____ provides the right to sell.

   a. Amortization
   b. AT'T Mobility LLC
   c. Annuity
   d. Option

Chapter 8. DEBT SECURITIES: THEORETICAL CONSIDERATIONS

1. _____ refers to a system of banking or banking activity that is consistent with the principles of Islamic law (Sharia) and its practical application through the development of Islamic economics. Sharia prohibits the payment of fees for the renting of money (Riba, usury) for specific terms, as well as investing in businesses that provide goods or services considered contrary to its principles (Haraam, forbidden.) While these principles were used as the basis for a flourishing economy in earlier times, it is only in the late 20th century that a number of Islamic banks were formed to apply these principles to private or semi-private commercial institutions within the Muslim community.
   a. ABN Amro
   b. A Random Walk Down Wall Street
   c. AAB
   d. Islamic banking

2. The _____ or redemption yield is the yield promised to the bondholder on the assumption that the bond or other fixed-interest security such as gilts will be held to maturity, that all coupon and principal payments will be made and coupon payments are reinvested at the bond's promised yield at the same rate as invested. It is a measure of the return of the bond. This technique in theory allows investors to calculate the fair value of different financial instruments.
   a. Yield
   b. 4-4-5 Calendar
   c. Macaulay duration
   d. Yield to maturity

3. In finance, the term _____ describes the amount in cash that returns to the owners of a security. Normally it does not include the price variations, at the difference of the total return. _____ applies to various stated rates of return on stocks (common and preferred, and convertible), fixed income instruments (bonds, notes, bills, strips, zero coupon), and some other investment type insurance products (e.g. annuities.)
   a. Yield
   b. 4-4-5 Calendar
   c. Yield to maturity
   d. Macaulay duration

4. _____ is a fee paid on borrowed assets. It is the price paid for the use of borrowed money , or, money earned by deposited funds . Assets that are sometimes lent with _____ include money, shares, consumer goods through hire purchase, major assets such as aircraft, and even entire factories in finance lease arrangements.
   a. Interest
   b. AAB
   c. Insolvency
   d. A Random Walk Down Wall Street

Chapter 8. DEBT SECURITIES: THEORETICAL CONSIDERATIONS   23

5. An _____ is the price a borrower pays for the use of money they do not own, and the return a lender receives for deferring the use of funds, by lending it to the borrower. _____s are normally expressed as a percentage rate over the period of one year.

_____s targets are also a vital tool of monetary policy and are used to control variables like investment, inflation, and unemployment.

   a. Interest rate
   b. ABN Amro
   c. A Random Walk Down Wall Street
   d. AAB

6. In finance, the yield curve is the relation between the interest rate (or cost of borrowing) and the time to maturity of the debt for a given borrower in a given currency. For example, the current U.S. dollar interest rates paid on U.S. Treasury securities for various maturities are closely watched by many traders, and are commonly plotted on a graph such as the one on the right which is informally called 'the yield curve.' More formal mathematical descriptions of this relation are often called the _____.

The yield of a debt instrument is the annualized percentage increase in the value of the investment.

   a. 529 plan
   b. Term structure of interest rates
   c. 4-4-5 Calendar
   d. 7-Eleven

7. The term _____ refers to three closely related concepts:

   - The _____ model is a mathematical model of the market for an equity, in which the equity's price is a stochastic process.
   - The _____ PDE is a partial differential equation which (in the model) must be satisfied by the price of a derivative on the equity.
   - The _____ formula is the result obtained by solving the _____ PDE for a European call option.

Fischer Black and Myron Scholes first articulated the _____ formula in their 1973 paper, 'The Pricing of Options and Corporate Liabilities.' The foundation for their research relied on work developed by scholars such as Jack L. Treynor, Paul Samuelson, A. James Boness, Sheen T. Kassouf, and Edward O. Thorp. The fundamental insight of _____ is that the option is implicitly priced if the stock is traded.

Robert C. Merton was the first to publish a paper expanding the mathematical understanding of the options pricing model and coined the term '_____' options pricing model.

Chapter 8. DEBT SECURITIES: THEORETICAL CONSIDERATIONS

a. Modified Internal Rate of Return
b. Stochastic volatility
c. Perpetuity
d. Black-Scholes

8. An _____ is a contract written by a seller that conveys to the buyer the right -- but not the obligation -- to buy (in the case of a call _____) or to sell (in the case of a put _____) a particular asset, such as a piece of property such as, among others, a futures contract. In return for granting the _____, the seller collects a payment (the premium) from the buyer.

For example, buying a call _____ provides the right to buy a specified quantity of a security at a set strike price at some time on or before expiration, while buying a put _____ provides the right to sell.

a. Amortization
b. AT'T Mobility LLC
c. Annuity
d. Option

9. In finance, a _____ is a debt security, in which the authorized issuer owes the holders a debt and, depending on the terms of the _____, is obliged to pay interest (the coupon) and/or to repay the principal at a later date, termed maturity.

Thus a _____ is a loan: the issuer is the borrower, the _____ holder is the lender, and the coupon is the interest. _____s provide the borrower with external funds to finance long-term investments, or, in the case of government _____s, to finance current expenditure.

a. Bond
b. Convertible bond
c. Catastrophe bonds
d. Puttable bond

10. The _____ or forward rate is the agreed upon price of an asset in a forward contract. Using the rational pricing assumption, we can express the _____ in terms of the spot price and any dividends etc., so that there is no possibility for arbitrage.

The _____ is given by:

Chapter 8. DEBT SECURITIES: THEORETICAL CONSIDERATIONS

where

    F is the _____ to be paid at time T
    e^x is the exponential function
    r is the risk-free interest rate
    q is the cost-of-carry
    S_0 is the spot price of the asset (i.e. what it would sell for at time 0)
    D_i is a dividend which is guaranteed to be paid at time t_i where $0 < t_i < T$.

The two questions here are what price the short position (the seller of the asset) should offer to maximize his gain, and what price the long position (the buyer of the asset) should accept to maximize his gain?

At the very least we know that both do not want to lose any money in the deal.

  a. Security interest
  b. Biweekly Mortgage
  c. Forward price
  d. Financial Gerontology

11. The _____ of a commodity, a security or a currency is the price that is quoted for immediate (spot) settlement (payment and delivery.) Spot settlement is normally one or two business days from trade date. This is in contrast with the forward price established in a forward contract or futures contract, where contract terms (price) are set now, but delivery and payment will occur at a future date.
  a. Spot rate
  b. Limits to arbitrage
  c. Market anomaly
  d. Long position

12. In finance, the _____ of a financial asset measures the sensitivity of the asset's price to interest rate movements, expressed as a number of years. The reason for expressing this sensitivity in years is that the time that will elapse until a cash flow is received allows more interest to accumulate. Therefore the price of an asset with long term cashflows has more interest rate sensitivity than an asset with cashflows in the near future.
  a. Yield to maturity
  b. 4-4-5 Calendar
  c. Duration
  d. Macaulay duration

Chapter 9. INTERNATIONAL PARITY RELATIONSHIPS

1. _____ refers to a system of banking or banking activity that is consistent with the principles of Islamic law (Sharia) and its practical application through the development of Islamic economics. Sharia prohibits the payment of fees for the renting of money (Riba, usury) for specific terms, as well as investing in businesses that provide goods or services considered contrary to its principles (Haraam, forbidden.) While these principles were used as the basis for a flourishing economy in earlier times, it is only in the late 20th century that a number of Islamic banks were formed to apply these principles to private or semi-private commercial institutions within the Muslim community.

   a. Islamic banking
   b. ABN Amro
   c. A Random Walk Down Wall Street
   d. AAB

2. In finance, the _____ between two currencies specifies how much one currency is worth in terms of the other. For example an _____ of 102 Japanese yen to the United States dollar means that JPY 102 is worth the same as USD 1. The foreign exchange market is one of the largest markets in the world.

   a. ABN Amro
   b. AAB
   c. A Random Walk Down Wall Street
   d. Exchange rate

3. The _____ is an economic law stated as: 'In an efficient market all identical goods must have only one price.'

   The intuition for this law is that all sellers will flock to the highest prevailing price, and all buyers to the lowest current market price. In an efficient market the convergence on one price is instant.

   Commodities can be traded on financial markets, where there will be a single offer price, and bid price.

   a. Letter of credit
   b. Personal property
   c. Liability
   d. Law of one price

4. _____ most frequently refers to the standard deviation of the continuously compounded returns of a financial instrument with a specific time horizon. It is often used to quantify the risk of the instrument over that time period. _____ is typically expressed in annualized terms, and it may either be an absolute number ($5) or a fraction of the mean (5%).

   a. Volatility
   b. Seasoned equity offering
   c. Currency swap
   d. Portfolio insurance

Chapter 9. INTERNATIONAL PARITY RELATIONSHIPS

5. _____ refers to a business or organization attempting to acquire goods or services to accomplish the goals of the enterprise. Though there are several organizations that attempt to set standards in the _____ process, processes can vary greatly between organizations. Typically the word '_____' is not used interchangeably with the word 'procurement', since procurement typically includes Expediting, Supplier Quality, and Traffic and Logistics (T'L) in addition to _____.
   a. Purchasing
   b. 529 plan
   c. 7-Eleven
   d. 4-4-5 Calendar

6. _____ is the value of goods/services compared to the amount paid with a currency. Currency can be either a commodity money, like gold or silver, or fiat currency like US dollars which are the world reserve currency. As Adam Smith noted, having money gives one the ability to 'command' others' labor, so _____ to some extent is power over other people, to the extent that they are willing to trade their labor or goods for money or currency.
   a. 529 plan
   b. 7-Eleven
   c. Purchasing power
   d. 4-4-5 Calendar

7. The _____ theory uses the long-term equilibrium exchange rate of two currencies to equalize their purchasing power. Developed by Gustav Cassel in 1920, it is based on the law of one price: the theory states that, in ideally efficient markets, identical goods should have only one price.

This purchasing power SEM rate equalizes the purchasing power of different currencies in their home countries for a given basket of goods.

   a. Gross national product
   b. TED spread
   c. 4-4-5 Calendar
   d. Purchasing power parity

8. _____ is a fee paid on borrowed assets. It is the price paid for the use of borrowed money , or, money earned by deposited funds . Assets that are sometimes lent with _____ include money, shares, consumer goods through hire purchase, major assets such as aircraft, and even entire factories in finance lease arrangements.
   a. A Random Walk Down Wall Street
   b. Insolvency
   c. AAB
   d. Interest

Chapter 9. INTERNATIONAL PARITY RELATIONSHIPS

9. An _____ is the price a borrower pays for the use of money they do not own, and the return a lender receives for deferring the use of funds, by lending it to the borrower. _____s are normally expressed as a percentage rate over the period of one year.

_____s targets are also a vital tool of monetary policy and are used to control variables like investment, inflation, and unemployment.

a. ABN Amro
b. A Random Walk Down Wall Street
c. AAB
d. Interest rate

10. _____ is an economic concept, expressed as a basic algebraic identity that relates interest rates and exchange rates. The identity is theoretical, and usually follows from assumptions imposed in economics models. There is evidence to support as well as to refute the concept.
a. A Random Walk Down Wall Street
b. Unit price
c. AAB
d. Interest rate parity

11. In economics, the _____ is the proposition by Irving Fisher that the real interest rate is independent of monetary measures, especially the nominal interest rate. The Fisher equation is

$$r_r = r_n >- >\pi^e.$$

This means, the real interest rate (r_r) equals the nominal interest rate (r_n) minus expected rate of inflation ($>\pi^e$.) Here all the rates are continuously compounded.

a. 4-4-5 Calendar
b. 7-Eleven
c. 529 plan
d. Fisher hypothesis

12. A _____ or market-based mechanism is any of a wide variety of ways to match up buyers and sellers.

An example of a _____ uses announced bid and ask prices. Generally speaking, when two parties wish to engage in a trade, the purchaser will announce a price he is willing to pay (the bid price) and seller will announce a price he is willing to accept (the ask price).

Chapter 9. INTERNATIONAL PARITY RELATIONSHIPS

a. Price mechanism
b. 7-Eleven
c. 4-4-5 Calendar
d. 529 plan

13. The _____ for securities is the difference between the price quoted by a market maker for an immediate sale and an immediate purchase The size of the bid-offer spread in a given commodity is a measure of the liquidity of the market.

The trader initiating the transaction is said to demand liquidity, and the other party to the transaction supplies liquidity.

a. Trade-off
b. Bid/offer spread
c. Defined contribution plan
d. Capital outflow

14. In economics, business, and accounting, a _____ is the value of money that has been used up to produce something, and hence is not available for use anymore. In business, the _____ may be one of acquisition, in which case the amount of money expended to acquire it is counted as _____. In this case, money is the input that is gone in order to acquire the thing.
a. Fixed costs
b. Marginal cost
c. Cost
d. Sliding scale fees

15. The _____ is a hypothesis in international finance that says that the difference in the nominal interest rates between two countries determines the movement of the nominal exchange rate between their currencies, with the value of the currency of the country with the lower nominal interest rate increasing. This is also known as the assumption of Uncovered Interest Parity.

The Fisher hypothesis says that the real interest rate in an economy is independent of monetary variables.

a. A Random Walk Down Wall Street
b. International Fisher effect
c. Official bank rate
d. Interest rate risk

16. In economics and related disciplines, a _____ is a cost incurred in making an economic exchange. For example, most people, when buying or selling a stock, must pay a commission to their broker; that commission is a _____ of doing the stock deal. Or consider buying a banana from a store; to purchase the banana, your costs will be not only the price of the banana itself, but also the energy and effort it requires to find out which of the various banana products you prefer, where to get them and at what price, the cost of traveling from your house to the store and back, the time waiting in line, and the effort of the paying itself; the costs above and beyond the cost of the banana are the _____s.
   a. Transaction cost
   b. Marginal cost
   c. Variable costs
   d. Fixed costs

Chapter 10. FOREIGN EXCHANGE

1. A _____ is an exchange of promises between two or more parties to do an act which is enforceable in a court of law. It is where an unqualified offer meets a qualified acceptance and the parties reach Consensus ad Idem. The parties must have the necessary capacity to _____ and the _____ must not be either trifling, indeterminate, impossible or illegal.
    a. 7-Eleven
    b. 529 plan
    c. 4-4-5 Calendar
    d. Contract

2. A _____ is an agreement between two parties to buy or sell an asset at a specified point of time in the future. The price of the underlying instrument, in whatever form, is paid before control of the instrument changes. This is one of the many forms of buy/sell orders where the time of trade is not the time where the securities themselves are exchanged.
    a. Constant maturity credit default swap
    b. Loan Credit Default Swap Index
    c. Derivatives markets
    d. Forward contract

3. In finance, a _____ is a derivative in which two counterparties agree to exchange one stream of cash flows against another stream. These streams are called the legs of the _____.

    The cash flows are calculated over a notional principal amount, which is usually not exchanged between counterparties.

    a. Local volatility
    b. Volatility swap
    c. Volatility arbitrage
    d. Swap

4. _____ refers to a system of banking or banking activity that is consistent with the principles of Islamic law (Sharia) and its practical application through the development of Islamic economics. Sharia prohibits the payment of fees for the renting of money (Riba, usury) for specific terms, as well as investing in businesses that provide goods or services considered contrary to its principles (Haraam, forbidden.) While these principles were used as the basis for a flourishing economy in earlier times, it is only in the late 20th century that a number of Islamic banks were formed to apply these principles to private or semi-private commercial institutions within the Muslim community.
    a. A Random Walk Down Wall Street
    b. ABN Amro
    c. Islamic banking
    d. AAB

Chapter 10. FOREIGN EXCHANGE

5. The _____ is where currency trading takes place. It is where banks and other official institutions facilitate the buying and selling of foreign currencies. FX transactions typically involve one party purchasing a quantity of one currency in exchange for paying a quantity of another.

   a. Spot market
   b. Foreign exchange option
   c. Floating exchange rate
   d. Foreign exchange market

6. _____ are a currency pair that does not include USD, such as GBP/JPY. Pairs that involve the EUR are called euro crosses, such as EUR/GBP. All other currency pairs (those that don't involve USD or EUR) are generally referred to as _____.

   a. Cross rates
   b. 4-4-5 Calendar
   c. 529 plan
   d. Foreign exchange risk

7. _____ is a fee paid on borrowed assets. It is the price paid for the use of borrowed money, or, money earned by deposited funds. Assets that are sometimes lent with _____ include money, shares, consumer goods through hire purchase, major assets such as aircraft, and even entire factories in finance lease arrangements.

   a. Insolvency
   b. A Random Walk Down Wall Street
   c. AAB
   d. Interest

8. An _____ is the price a borrower pays for the use of money they do not own, and the return a lender receives for deferring the use of funds, by lending it to the borrower. _____s are normally expressed as a percentage rate over the period of one year.

   _____s targets are also a vital tool of monetary policy and are used to control variables like investment, inflation, and unemployment.

   a. ABN Amro
   b. AAB
   c. Interest rate
   d. A Random Walk Down Wall Street

Chapter 10. FOREIGN EXCHANGE

9. _____ is an economic concept, expressed as a basic algebraic identity that relates interest rates and exchange rates. The identity is theoretical, and usually follows from assumptions imposed in economics models. There is evidence to support as well as to refute the concept.
  a. A Random Walk Down Wall Street
  b. Unit price
  c. AAB
  d. Interest rate parity

10. _____ most frequently refers to the standard deviation of the continuously compounded returns of a financial instrument with a specific time horizon. It is often used to quantify the risk of the instrument over that time period. _____ is typically expressed in annualized terms, and it may either be an absolute number ($5) or a fraction of the mean (5%).
  a. Seasoned equity offering
  b. Currency swap
  c. Portfolio insurance
  d. Volatility

Chapter 11. MARKOWITZ AND THE CAPITAL ASSET PRICING MODEL

1. _____ proposes how rational investors will use diversification to optimize their portfolios, and how a risky asset should be priced. The basic concepts of the theory are Markowitz diversification, the efficient frontier, capital asset pricing model, the alpha and beta coefficients, the Capital Market Line and the Securities Market Line.

_____ models an asset's return as a random variable, and models a portfolio as a weighted combination of assets so that the return of a portfolio is the weighted combination of the assets' returns.

   a. Payback period
   b. Market value
   c. Consumer basket
   d. Modern portfolio theory

2. _____ most frequently refers to the standard deviation of the continuously compounded returns of a financial instrument with a specific time horizon. It is often used to quantify the risk of the instrument over that time period. _____ is typically expressed in annualized terms, and it may either be an absolute number ($5) or a fraction of the mean (5%).
   a. Currency swap
   b. Seasoned equity offering
   c. Portfolio insurance
   d. Volatility

3. Modern portfolio theory (MPT) proposes how rational investors will use diversification to optimize their portfolios, and how a risky asset should be priced. The basic concepts of the theory are Markowitz diversification, the _____, capital asset pricing model, the alpha and beta coefficients, the Capital Market Line and the Securities Market Line.

MPT models an asset's return as a random variable, and models a portfolio as a weighted combination of assets so that the return of a portfolio is the weighted combination of the assets' returns.

   a. AAB
   b. A Random Walk Down Wall Street
   c. ABN Amro
   d. Efficient frontier

4. _____ in finance is a risk management technique, related to hedging, that mixes a wide variety of investments within a portfolio. Because the fluctuations of a single security have less impact on a diverse portfolio, _____ minimizes the risk from any one investment.

A simple example of _____ is the following: On a particular island the entire economy consists of two companies: one that sells umbrellas and another that sells sunscreen.

a. 7-Eleven
b. 529 plan
c. 4-4-5 Calendar
d. Diversification

5. _____ refers to a system of banking or banking activity that is consistent with the principles of Islamic law (Sharia) and its practical application through the development of Islamic economics. Sharia prohibits the payment of fees for the renting of money (Riba, usury) for specific terms, as well as investing in businesses that provide goods or services considered contrary to its principles (Haraam, forbidden.) While these principles were used as the basis for a flourishing economy in earlier times, it is only in the late 20th century that a number of Islamic banks were formed to apply these principles to private or semi-private commercial institutions within the Muslim community.
  a. ABN Amro
  b. AAB
  c. Islamic banking
  d. A Random Walk Down Wall Street

6. _____ is the planning process used to determine whether a firm's long term investments such as new machinery, replacement machinery, new plants, new products, and research development projects are worth pursuing. It is budget for major capital, or investment, expenditures.

Many formal methods are used in _____, including the techniques such as

- Net present value
- Profitability index
- Internal rate of return
- Modified Internal Rate of Return
- Equivalent annuity

These methods use the incremental cash flows from each potential investment, or project. Techniques based on accounting earnings and accounting rules are sometimes used - though economists consider this to be improper - such as the accounting rate of return, and 'return on investment.' Simplified and hybrid methods are used as well, such as payback period and discounted payback period.

  a. Financial distress
  b. Capital budgeting
  c. Shareholder value
  d. Preferred stock

Chapter 11. MARKOWITZ AND THE CAPITAL ASSET PRICING MODEL

7. In business and accounting, _____s are everything of value that is owned by a person or company. The balance sheet of a firm records the monetary value of the _____s owned by the firm. The two major _____ classes are tangible _____s and intangible _____s.
   a. EBITDA
   b. Accounts payable
   c. Asset
   d. Income

8. In finance, _____ is the process of estimating the potential market value of a financial asset or liability. they can be done on assets (for example, investments in marketable securities such as stocks, options, business enterprises, or intangible assets such as patents and trademarks) or on liabilities (e.g., Bonds issued by a company.) _____s are required in many contexts including investment analysis, capital budgeting, merger and acquisition transactions, financial reporting, taxable events to determine the proper tax liability, and in litigation.
   a. Margin
   b. Procter ' Gamble
   c. Share
   d. Valuation

9. The term _____ has three unrelated technical definitions, and is also used in a variety of non-technical ways.

   - In financial economics, it refers to any asset used to make money, as opposed to assets used for personal enjoyment or consumption. This is an important distinction because two people can disagree sharply about the value of personal assets, one person might think a sports car is more valuable than a pickup truck, another person might have the opposite taste. But if an asset is held for the purpose of making money, taste has nothing to do with it, only differences of opinion about how much money the asset will produce. With the further assumption that people agree on the probability distribution of future cash flows, it is possible to have an objective _____ pricing model. Even without the assumption of agreement, it is possible to set rational limits on _____ value.
   - In governmental accounting, it is defined as any asset used in operations with an initial useful life extending beyond one reporting period. Generally, government managers have a 'stewardship' duty to maintain _____s under their control. See International Public Sector Accounting Standards for details.
   - In US tax accounting, it is defined as any property other than a list of exceptions. The main exceptions are anything held for sale, and any real estate or depreciable property used in business. Almost everything you own and use for personal purposes, pleasure or investment is a _____. If something is a _____ for tax purposes, gains or losses on sale or disposition are capital gains or capital losses. For individuals, however, capital losses on property held for personal use are generally not deductible. See the IRS publication Tax Facts about Capital Gains and Losses for details.

A well-known financial accounting textbook advises that the term be avoided except in tax accounting because it is used in so many different senses, not all of them well-defined. For example it is often used as a synonym for fixed assets or for investments in securities.

Chapter 11. MARKOWITZ AND THE CAPITAL ASSET PRICING MODEL

A common non-technical usage occurs when people ask that employees or the environment or something else be treated as a _____.

a. Solvency
b. Settlement date
c. Political risk
d. Capital asset

10. In finance, the _____ is used to determine a theoretically appropriate required rate of return of an asset, if that asset is to be added to an already well-diversified portfolio, given that asset's non-diversifiable risk. The model takes into account the asset's sensitivity to non-diversifiable risk (also known as systemic risk or market risk), often represented by the quantity beta (β) in the financial industry, as well as the expected return of the market and the expected return of a theoretical risk-free asset.

The model was introduced by Jack Treynor (1961, 1962), William Sharpe (1964), John Lintner (1965a,b) and Jan Mossin (1966) independently, building on the earlier work of Harry Markowitz on diversification and modern portfolio theory.

a. Random walk hypothesis
b. Hull-White model
c. Cox-Ingersoll-Ross model
d. Capital asset pricing model

11. An _____ or index tracker is a collective investment scheme (usually a mutual fund or exchange-traded fund) that aims to replicate the movements of an index of a specific financial market regardless of market conditions.

Tracking can be achieved by trying to hold all of the securities in the index, in the same proportions as the index. Other methods include statistically sampling the market and holding 'representative' securities.

a. Index fund
b. A Random Walk Down Wall Street
c. Investment company
d. AAB

Chapter 12. FUTURES

1. A _____ is an exchange of promises between two or more parties to do an act which is enforceable in a court of law. It is where an unqualified offer meets a qualified acceptance and the parties reach Consensus ad Idem. The parties must have the necessary capacity to _____ and the _____ must not be either trifling, indeterminate, impossible or illegal.

   a. 529 plan
   b. 7-Eleven
   c. 4-4-5 Calendar
   d. Contract

2. _____ refers to a system of banking or banking activity that is consistent with the principles of Islamic law (Sharia) and its practical application through the development of Islamic economics. Sharia prohibits the payment of fees for the renting of money (Riba, usury) for specific terms, as well as investing in businesses that provide goods or services considered contrary to its principles (Haraam, forbidden.) While these principles were used as the basis for a flourishing economy in earlier times, it is only in the late 20th century that a number of Islamic banks were formed to apply these principles to private or semi-private commercial institutions within the Muslim community.

   a. AAB
   b. A Random Walk Down Wall Street
   c. ABN Amro
   d. Islamic banking

3. A _____ is a financial services company that provides clearing and settlement services for financial transactions, usually on a futures exchange, and often acts as central counterparty (the payor actually pays the _____, which then pays the payee). A _____ may also offer novation, the substitution of a new contract or debt for an old, or other credit enhancement services to its members.

   The term is also used for banks like Suffolk Bank that acted as a restraint on the over-issuance of private bank notes.

   a. Bucket shop
   b. Clearing house
   c. Warrant
   d. Valuation

4. _____ is a fee paid on borrowed assets. It is the price paid for the use of borrowed money , or, money earned by deposited funds . Assets that are sometimes lent with _____ include money, shares, consumer goods through hire purchase, major assets such as aircraft, and even entire factories in finance lease arrangements.

Chapter 12. FUTURES

a. A Random Walk Down Wall Street
b. Insolvency
c. AAB
d. Interest

5. _____ denotes the total number of derivative contracts, like futures and options, that are currently active on a specific underlying security, having specific terms.

Namely, the total contracts for a specific strike price and expiration date, that have been traded, but have not yet expired, have not yet been closed through a closing transaction, or have not yet been terminated via early exercise. A closing transaction occurs when a counterparty that longs the contract sells, or, conversely, when a counterparty that shorts the contract buys.

a. Open interest
b. Equity swap
c. International Swaps and Derivatives Association
d. Equity derivative

6. _____ is the name of a method of communication between professionals on a stock exchange or futures exchange which involves shouting and the use of hand signals to transfer information primarily about buy and sell orders. The part of the trading floor where this takes place is called a pit.

Examples of markets which use this system in the United States are the New York Mercantile Exchange, the Chicago Mercantile Exchange, the Chicago Board of Trade, and the Chicago Board Options Exchange.

a. Open outcry
b. Insider trading
c. Equity investment
d. Intellidex

7. In finance, a _____ is collateral that the holder of a position in securities, options, or futures contracts has to deposit to cover the credit risk of his counterparty (most often his broker.) This risk can arise if the holder has done any of the following:

- borrowed cash from the counterparty to buy securities or options,
- sold securities or options short, or
- entered into a futures contract.

The collateral can be in the form of cash or securities, and it is deposited in a _____ account. On U.S. futures exchanges, '_____' was formally called performance bond.

Chapter 12. FUTURES

_____ buying is buying securities with cash borrowed from a broker, using other securities as collateral.

a. Procter ' Gamble
b. Credit
c. Share
d. Margin

8. In finance, a _____ is a standardized contract, to buy or sell a specified commodity of standardized quality at a certain date in the future, at a market determined price (the futures price.)

The price is determined by the instantaneous equilibrium between the forces of supply and demand among competing buy and sell orders on the exchange at the time of the purchase or sale of the contract.

In many cases, the items may be such non-traditional 'commodities' as foreign currencies, commercial or government paper [e.g., bonds], or 'baskets' of corporate equity ['stock indices'] or other financial instruments.

a. Financial future
b. Heston model
c. Futures contract
d. Repurchase agreement

9. The _____ of an asset is the return obtained from holding it (if positive), or the cost of holding it (if negative)

For instance, commodities are usually negative _____ assets, as they incur storage costs, but in some circumstances, commodities can be positive _____ assets as the market is willing to pay a premium for availability.

This can also refer to a trade with more than one leg, where you earn the spread between borrowing a low _____ asset and lending a high _____ one.

a. Cramdown
b. Carry
c. Financial assistance
d. Bankruptcy remote

Chapter 12. FUTURES

10. In economics, business, and accounting, a _____ is the value of money that has been used up to produce something, and hence is not available for use anymore. In business, the _____ may be one of acquisition, in which case the amount of money expended to acquire it is counted as _____. In this case, money is the input that is gone in order to acquire the thing.
    a. Fixed costs
    b. Marginal cost
    c. Sliding scale fees
    d. Cost

11. The _____ is the cost of 'carrying' or holding a position. If long, the _____ is the cost of interest paid on a margin account. Conversely, if short, the _____ is the cost of paying dividends, or opportunity cost the cost of purchasing a particular security rather than an alternative.
    a. Delta hedging
    b. Secondary market
    c. Spot price
    d. Cost of carry

12. A _____ is an agreement between two parties to buy or sell an asset at a specified point of time in the future. The price of the underlying instrument, in whatever form, is paid before control of the instrument changes. This is one of the many forms of buy/sell orders where the time of trade is not the time where the securities themselves are exchanged.
    a. Forward contract
    b. Constant maturity credit default swap
    c. Derivatives markets
    d. Loan Credit Default Swap Index

13. The _____ or spot rate of a commodity, a security or a currency is the price that is quoted for immediate (spot) settlement (payment and delivery.) Spot settlement is normally one or two business days from trade date. This is in contrast with the forward price established in a forward contract or futures contract, where contract terms (price) are set now, but delivery and payment will occur at a future date.
    a. Spot price
    b. Central Securities Depository
    c. Market price
    d. Cost of carry

14. _____ most frequently refers to the standard deviation of the continuously compounded returns of a financial instrument with a specific time horizon. It is often used to quantify the risk of the instrument over that time period. _____ is typically expressed in annualized terms, and it may either be an absolute number ($5) or a fraction of the mean (5%).

a. Currency swap
b. Volatility
c. Portfolio insurance
d. Seasoned equity offering

Chapter 13. OPTIONS

1. An _____ is a contract written by a seller that conveys to the buyer the right -- but not the obligation -- to buy (in the case of a call _____) or to sell (in the case of a put _____) a particular asset, such as a piece of property such as, among others, a futures contract. In return for granting the _____, the seller collects a payment (the premium) from the buyer.

For example, buying a call _____ provides the right to buy a specified quantity of a security at a set strike price at some time on or before expiration, while buying a put _____ provides the right to sell.

   a. Option
   b. Annuity
   c. Amortization
   d. AT'T Mobility LLC

2. In financial mathematics, _____ defines a relationship between the price of a call option and a put option--both with the identical strike price and expiry. To derive the _____ relationship, the assumption is that the options are not exercised before expiration day, which necessarily applies to European options. _____ can be derived in a manner that is largely model independent.
   a. Cox-Ingersoll-Ross model
   b. Rendleman-Bartter model
   c. Put-call parity
   d. Hull-White model

3. _____ most frequently refers to the standard deviation of the continuously compounded returns of a financial instrument with a specific time horizon. It is often used to quantify the risk of the instrument over that time period. _____ is typically expressed in annualized terms, and it may either be an absolute number ($5) or a fraction of the mean (5%).
   a. Seasoned equity offering
   b. Portfolio insurance
   c. Currency swap
   d. Volatility

4. The term _____ refers to three closely related concepts:

   - The _____ model is a mathematical model of the market for an equity, in which the equity's price is a stochastic process.
   - The _____ PDE is a partial differential equation which (in the model) must be satisfied by the price of a derivative on the equity.
   - The _____ formula is the result obtained by solving the _____ PDE for a European call option.

Chapter 13. OPTIONS

Fischer Black and Myron Scholes first articulated the _____ formula in their 1973 paper, 'The Pricing of Options and Corporate Liabilities.' The foundation for their research relied on work developed by scholars such as Jack L. Treynor, Paul Samuelson, A. James Boness, Sheen T. Kassouf, and Edward O. Thorp. The fundamental insight of _____ is that the option is implicitly priced if the stock is traded.

Robert C. Merton was the first to publish a paper expanding the mathematical understanding of the options pricing model and coined the term '_____' options pricing model.

   a. Modified Internal Rate of Return
   b. Black-Scholes
   c. Perpetuity
   d. Stochastic volatility

5. In finance, the binomial options pricing model (BOPM) provides a generalisable numerical method for the valuation of options. The _____ was first proposed by Cox, Ross and Rubinstein (1979.) Essentially, the model uses a 'discrete-time' model of the varying price over time of the underlying financial instrument.
   a. Discount rate
   b. Perpetuity
   c. Modified Internal Rate of Return
   d. Binomial model

Chapter 14. SWAPS

1. _____ is a fee paid on borrowed assets. It is the price paid for the use of borrowed money, or, money earned by deposited funds. Assets that are sometimes lent with _____ include money, shares, consumer goods through hire purchase, major assets such as aircraft, and even entire factories in finance lease arrangements.
   a. A Random Walk Down Wall Street
   b. Interest
   c. AAB
   d. Insolvency

2. An _____ is the price a borrower pays for the use of money they do not own, and the return a lender receives for deferring the use of funds, by lending it to the borrower. _____s are normally expressed as a percentage rate over the period of one year.

   _____s targets are also a vital tool of monetary policy and are used to control variables like investment, inflation, and unemployment.

   a. Interest rate
   b. A Random Walk Down Wall Street
   c. ABN Amro
   d. AAB

3. A _____ is something for which there is demand, but which is supplied without qualitative differentiation across a market. It is a product that is the same no matter who produces it, such as petroleum, notebook paper, or milk. In other words, copper is copper.
   a. 529 plan
   b. Commodity
   c. 4-4-5 Calendar
   d. 7-Eleven

4. In finance, a _____ is a derivative in which two counterparties agree to exchange one stream of cash flows against another stream. These streams are called the legs of the _____.

   The cash flows are calculated over a notional principal amount, which is usually not exchanged between counterparties.

   a. Swap
   b. Local volatility
   c. Volatility swap
   d. Volatility arbitrage

Chapter 14. SWAPS

5. A _____ is an option granting its owner the right but not the obligation to enter into an underlying swap. Although options can be traded on a variety of swaps, the term '_____' typically refers to options on interest rate swaps.

There are two types of _____ contracts:

- A payer _____ gives the owner of the _____ the right to enter into a swap where they pay the fixed leg and receive the floating leg.
- A receiver _____ gives the owner of the _____ the right to enter into a swap where they will receive the fixed leg, and pay the floating leg.

The buyer and seller of the _____ agree on:

- the premium (price) of the _____
- the strike rate (equal to the fixed rate of the underlying swap)
- length of the option period (which usually ends two business days prior to the start date of the underlying swap),
- the term of the underlying swap,
- notional amount,
- amortization, if any
- frequency of settlement of payments on the underlying swap

The participants in the _____ market are predominantly large corporations, banks, financial institutions and hedge funds. End users such as corporations and banks typically use _____s to manage interest rate risk arising from their core business or from their financing arrangements.

a. Swaption
b. Put option
c. Straddle
d. Bear call spread

6. In finance, _____ is the process of estimating the potential market value of a financial asset or liability. they can be done on assets (for example, investments in marketable securities such as stocks, options, business enterprises, or intangible assets such as patents and trademarks) or on liabilities (e.g., Bonds issued by a company.) _____s are required in many contexts including investment analysis, capital budgeting, merger and acquisition transactions, financial reporting, taxable events to determine the proper tax liability, and in litigation.
a. Share
b. Valuation
c. Procter ' Gamble
d. Margin

Chapter 15. HEDGING

1. In finance, a _____ is a position established in one market in an attempt to offset exposure to the price risk of an equal but opposite obligation or position in another market -- usually, but not always, in the context of one's commercial activity. Hedging is a strategy designed to minimize exposure to such business risks as a sharp contraction in demand for one's inventory, while still allowing the business to profit from producing and maintaining that inventory. A typical hedger might be a farmer with 2000 acres of unharvested wheat in the ground, who would rather tend his crop without the distraction of uncertain prices.
   a. 7-Eleven
   b. 529 plan
   c. 4-4-5 Calendar
   d. Hedge

2. In finance, a _____ is a standardized contract, to buy or sell a specified commodity of standardized quality at a certain date in the future, at a market determined price (the futures price.)

   The price is determined by the instantaneous equilibrium between the forces of supply and demand among competing buy and sell orders on the exchange at the time of the purchase or sale of the contract.

   In many cases, the items may be such non-traditional 'commodities' as foreign currencies, commercial or government paper [e.g., bonds], or 'baskets' of corporate equity ['stock indices'] or other financial instruments.

   a. Heston model
   b. Repurchase agreement
   c. Financial future
   d. Futures contract

3. An _____ is a contract written by a seller that conveys to the buyer the right -- but not the obligation -- to buy (in the case of a call _____) or to sell (in the case of a put _____) a particular asset, such as a piece of property such as, among others, a futures contract. In return for granting the _____, the seller collects a payment (the premium) from the buyer.

   For example, buying a call _____ provides the right to buy a specified quantity of a security at a set strike price at some time on or before expiration, while buying a put _____ provides the right to sell.

   a. Amortization
   b. Annuity
   c. AT'T Mobility LLC
   d. Option

4. A _____ is a fungible, negotiable instrument representing financial value. They are broadly categorized into debt securities (such as banknotes, bonds and debentures), and equity securities; e.g., common stocks. The company or other entity issuing the _____ is called the issuer.

Chapter 15. HEDGING

a. Securities lending
b. Security
c. Book entry
d. Tracking stock

5. A _____ is a private investment fund open to a limited range of investors that is permitted by regulators to undertake a wider range of activities than other investment funds and also pays a performance fee to its investment manager. Each fund will have its own strategy which determines the type of investments and the methods of investment it undertakes. _____s as a class invest in a broad range of investments extending over shares, debt, commodities and beyond.

a. 4-4-5 Calendar
b. 529 plan
c. 7-Eleven
d. Hedge fund

6. A _____ or market-based mechanism is any of a wide variety of ways to match up buyers and sellers.

An example of a _____ uses announced bid and ask prices. Generally speaking, when two parties wish to engage in a trade, the purchaser will announce a price he is willing to pay (the bid price) and seller will announce a price he is willing to accept (the ask price).

a. 529 plan
b. 4-4-5 Calendar
c. 7-Eleven
d. Price mechanism

7. The _____ for securities is the difference between the price quoted by a market maker for an immediate sale and an immediate purchase The size of the bid-offer spread in a given commodity is a measure of the liquidity of the market.

The trader initiating the transaction is said to demand liquidity, and the other party to the transaction supplies liquidity.

a. Capital outflow
b. Trade-off
c. Defined contribution plan
d. Bid/offer spread

Chapter 15. HEDGING

8. In economics, business, and accounting, a _____ is the value of money that has been used up to produce something, and hence is not available for use anymore. In business, the _____ may be one of acquisition, in which case the amount of money expended to acquire it is counted as _____. In this case, money is the input that is gone in order to acquire the thing.
    a. Sliding scale fees
    b. Marginal cost
    c. Fixed costs
    d. Cost

9. In economics and related disciplines, a _____ is a cost incurred in making an economic exchange. For example, most people, when buying or selling a stock, must pay a commission to their broker; that commission is a _____ of doing the stock deal. Or consider buying a banana from a store; to purchase the banana, your costs will be not only the price of the banana itself, but also the energy and effort it requires to find out which of the various banana products you prefer, where to get them and at what price, the cost of traveling from your house to the store and back, the time waiting in line, and the effort of the paying itself; the costs above and beyond the cost of the banana are the _____s.
    a. Transaction cost
    b. Marginal cost
    c. Variable costs
    d. Fixed costs

10. In financial mathematics and financial risk management, _____ is a widely used measure of the risk of loss on a specific portfolio of financial assets. For a given portfolio, probability and time horizon, VaR is defined as a threshold value such that the probability that the mark-to-market loss on the portfolio over the given time horizon exceeds this value (assuming normal markets and no trading) is the given probability level.

    For example, if a portfolio of stocks has a one-day 5% VaR of $1 million, there is a 5% probability that the portfolio will fall in value by more than $1 million over a one day period, assuming markets are normal and there is no trading.

    a. Discount factor
    b. Risk modeling
    c. Risk aversion
    d. Value at risk

11. When companies conduct business across borders, they must deal in foreign currencies. Companies must exchange foreign currencies for home currencies when dealing with receivables, and vice versa for payables. This is done at the current exchange rate between the two countries. _____ is the risk that the exchange rate will change unfavorably before the currency is exchanged.

a. 4-4-5 Calendar
b. 529 plan
c. Lower of cost or market rule
d. Foreign exchange risk

ANSWER KEY

Chapter 1
1. b   2. c   3. d   4. d   5. d   6. d   7. d   8. d   9. b   10. c
11. d   12. b   13. d   14. c   15. d   16. c   17. d

Chapter 2
1. d   2. c   3. a   4. d   5. d   6. c   7. d   8. a   9. d   10. d
11. b   12. c   13. d

Chapter 3
1. b   2. d   3. d   4. d   5. a   6. a

Chapter 4
1. c   2. d   3. a   4. d   5. d

Chapter 5
1. c   2. b   3. c   4. d   5. d

Chapter 6
1. b   2. d   3. b   4. d   5. b   6. d   7. c   8. b   9. a   10. c
11. d   12. d   13. d

Chapter 7
1. d   2. d   3. d   4. d   5. d   6. d

Chapter 8
1. d   2. d   3. a   4. a   5. a   6. b   7. d   8. d   9. a   10. c
11. a   12. c

Chapter 9
1. a   2. d   3. d   4. a   5. a   6. c   7. d   8. d   9. d   10. d
11. d   12. a   13. b   14. c   15. b   16. a

Chapter 10
1. d   2. d   3. d   4. c   5. d   6. a   7. d   8. c   9. d   10. d

Chapter 11
1. d   2. d   3. d   4. d   5. c   6. b   7. c   8. d   9. d   10. d
11. a

Chapter 12
1. d   2. d   3. b   4. d   5. a   6. a   7. d   8. c   9. b   10. d
11. d   12. a   13. a   14. b

Chapter 13
1. a   2. c   3. d   4. b   5. d

Chapter 14
1. b   2. a   3. b   4. a   5. a   6. b

Chapter 15
1. d   2. d   3. d   4. b   5. d   6. d   7. d   8. d   9. a   10. d
11. d